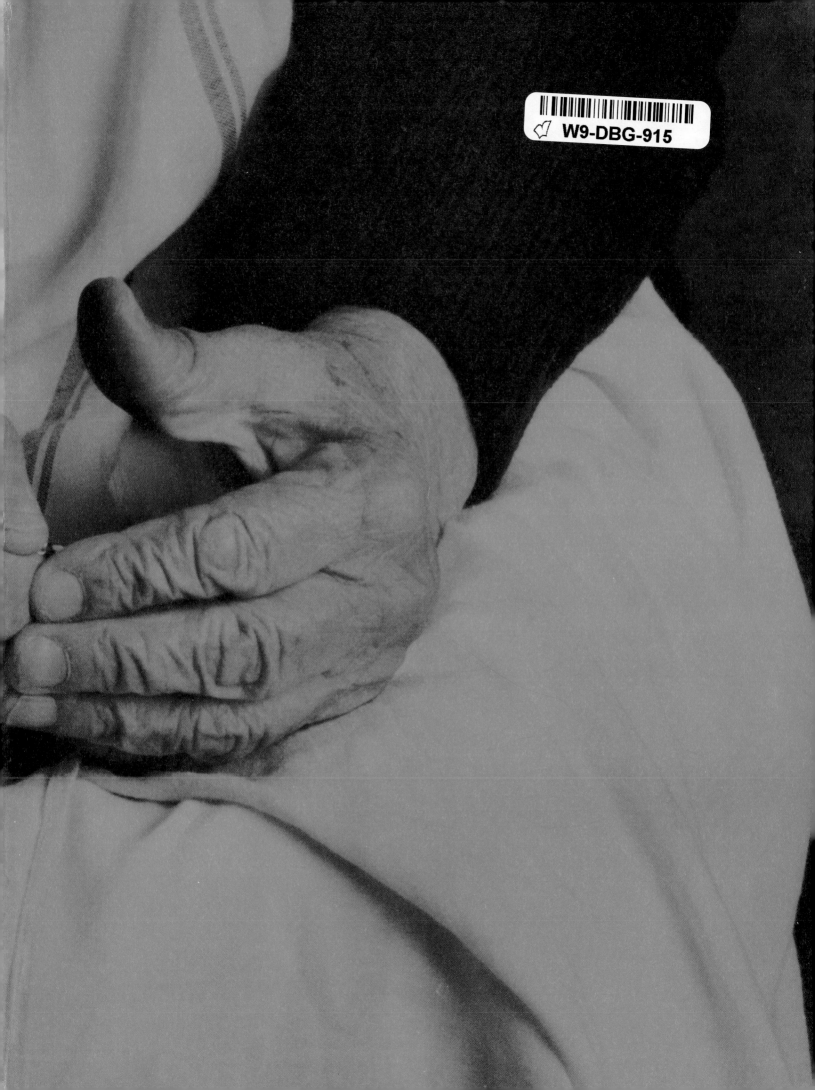

MOTHER TERESA OF CALCUTTA

'One day I was walking down the streets of London and I saw a man quite drunk. He was looking so sad and miserable I went right up to him and took his hand, shook it and asked, "How are you?" My hand is always warm – and he said, "Oh, after so long I feel the warmth of a human hand." And his face lit up. And his face was different. I only want to say that small things done in great love bring joy and peace.'

MOTHER TERESA
OF CALCUTTA

SUNITA KUMAR

IGNATIUS PRESS   SAN FRANCISCO

First published in Great Britain in 1998

by Weidenfeld & Nicolson

Text copyright © Sunita Kumar, 1998

The moral right of Sunita Kumar to be identified as the author of this work has been

asserted in accordance with the Copyright, Designs and Patents Act of 1988

Design and layout copyright © Weidenfeld & Nicolson, 1998

Photographs have kindly been supplied by the following:
p. 103 © Ananda/Outlook; p. 114, 115 © Ahmed Ali; p. 2, 31, 63, 69, 75(b), 77, 106 ©
Tarapada Banerjee; endpapers, p. 6, 50, 51(t), 70 © Carlo & Ciro; p. 1, 19, 59, 119 ©
Michael Collopy; p. 48(t), 62(t) © Amit Datta; p. 12, 17, 49, 96 © Sunita Kumar;
p. 29, 36, 38, 54, 79(t), 84 © Sunil Kumar Dutt/Camera Press; p. 20, 21, 26, 27(t&b) ©
Agi Guttaduaro Mancinelli; p. 86, 92 © Sandy McMurtrie; p. 13 © Derry Moore; p. 79(b),
81(t&b), 82(t&b), 85, 87(t&b), 88, 89, 90 © L'Osservatore Romano; p. 40, 83(t), 93, 94, 97,
99, 100, 101, 102, 104, 107, 109, 111, 112, 113 © Ananda Bazaar Patrika; p. 14 © Petrie
Productions; p. 16, 22, 23, 25, 48(b) © Private Collection; p. 34, 35(t&b), 37, 41, 75(t), 108,
110 © Moriho Oki; p. 9, 11, 33, 43, 44(t), 55, 61, 66, 72, 74, 76 © Raghu Rai; p. 98 ©
Jayanta Shaw; p. 62(b), 83(b), 91, 105 © *The Statesman*, Calcutta; p. 39(t&b), 42, 44(b), 45,
46(t&b), 47, 51(b), 52, 53, 56, 57, 58, 60, 65(t&b), 67, 68–9, 71, 73 © Jay Ullal/Stern.

ISBN 0-89870-729-3

Designed by: Leigh Jones

Set in: Futura Book

Printed in Great Britain

Co-published with

Weidenfeld & Nicolson

The Orion Publishing Group Ltd

5 Upper St Martin's Lane

London WC2H 9EA

CONTENTS

ACKNOWLEDGEMENTS

At the final professions in Rome on 24 May 1997. After the ceremony the sisters are welcomed by the novices.

If it wasn't for the support I received from the sisters I would never have had the courage to go ahead and write this book. When I first discussed the idea with Sister Priscilla she encouraged me to talk to Sister Nirmala about it; she too liked the idea and blessed the project. All the sisters have been very helpful but I would like to especially thank Sister Nirmala, Sister Frederick, Sister Priscilla, Sister Lysa, Sister Martin de Porres, Sister Joel, Sister Christie (Calcutta), Sister Elena, Sister Gertrude (Rome) and Sister Terrasina (London) for their unstinting support.

My sincere thanks to Mother's niece Agi, who always responded with much love and affection to my frequent requests for family photographs and other information.

I am most grateful to Aveek Sarkar of the Ananda Bazaar Group, Cushrow Irani of *The Statesman*, R. P. Gupta and Sandy McMurtrie who all went out of their way to help me. My thanks is also due to Michael Dover, Claire Wedderburn-Maxwell and Leigh Jones who produced the book.

Many thanks to my son Arjun and his wife Jessima for their help, and to my husband Naresh who has always encouraged me in everything that I have set out to do and who helped me see this book through.

Saying thank you to those who have given their photographs is not enough. The beautiful photographs from Raghu Rai, Michael Collopy, Morihiro Oki, Jay Ullal (Stern), Tarapada Banerjee, Amit Dutta, L'Osservatore Romano, Carlo & Ciro, Jayanta Shaw, Ananda Bazaar Patrika, *The Statesman* and Outlook/Ananda, have captured some of the most wonderful moments of Mother's life. Their prompt and generous response to my requests for photographs was overwhelming. They are as much a part of this book as I am, and we have all done this together for the love of Mother and her work, and that is how she would have liked it.

54A A.J.C. Bose Road
Calcutta 700016 INDIA

"As long as you did it to one of these My least brethren. You did it to Me"

23.5.1998

Dear Sunita,

Thank you very much for all the love and
enthusiasm you have put in preparing this work of
love to commemorate the first anniversary of our
dearest Mother's going home to God.

May this bring many blessings on you, on your
family, on those who have contributed the photographs
and all those who will just look at or read your
little book.

May this coming in contact with Mother
rekindle the fire of love in each heart, for God and
for His children, especially the poorest of the
poor.

We, Missionaries of Charity, will always
remain grateful to you for all you have been to our
Mother and to us all these years.

God bless you

M. Nirmala M.C.

Letter of Blessing from Sister Nirmala

INTRODUCTION

In 1967 I joined the Co-Workers of Mother Teresa, volunteers who met once a week to roll bandages and pack pills into special paper packets for the leprosy patients. It was at one such get-together that I first met Mother Teresa. She had a beautiful smile, she was cheerful, and I found a strange warmth filling my whole being as I shook her hand. I loved her at first sight. She did not demand or preach. On the contrary, she was like a friend in an informal gathering. She spoke softly to me. Her voice was rich and deep. It occurs to me now that, in all these years, not once did I hear her raise her voice. When necessary, she would merely speak in a firm tone.

Mother's life was unique. She lived very simply and humbly like the poor. For example, in Mother's house the only room that has a fan is the parlour, and that is used for the visitors. Her room was in the worst location, just above the kitchen. With the heat rising from the kitchen into her room it must have been unbearable in the height of summer. Her room was small, approximately twelve foot by eight, with only one window. She had a small table and a stool that served as a chair. It was at this table that she did all her work for her 595 homes. She would work until late at night; normally she slept for five or six hours and had a half-hour nap in the afternoon. She insisted on keeping the telephone in her room and always answered all the calls herself if she was at home, with her usual 'Yes'.

Her diet was frugal and similar to what the poor in Calcutta would eat. Initially she used to have just a chapati and dhal (lentils) or vegetables for her meal. Mother Dengal, who was the doctor and head of the Medical Missionaries in Patna, where Mother went for her training, advised her against it. 'If you get sick, how will you serve the poor?' she asked. She listened to Mother Dengal and started having a chapati, a little vegetable oil, a cup of tea and a banana for her breakfast. For lunch

RIGHT
Receiving an award
in Madras in 1989.

With the Kumar family at Shishu Bhawan. She had a good sense of humour, often making witty remarks, and when amused she would double up with laughter.

RIGHT
With the author in 1988.

she would have rice and watery curry (a poor person's curry) without any of the tasty spices. The curry would be either vegetable and egg, vegetable with lentils or occasionally meat and vegetable. The evening meal was always kedgeree (rice and lentils cooked together with some vegetables). Occasionally she would have fruit (onions and cucumbers are also considered to be fruit). This became the standard diet for all the sisters.

Her overseas trips were always hectic. She travelled a lot but there was never any jet lag or fuss. She had very little time for herself, sometimes working until 2 a.m. I remember on one of our trips together, I gave up after two days. I just couldn't keep up with the pace. 'Mother, I just can't do any more, how do you carry on?' I asked. 'I fill my tank with prayer,' she said.

In spite of working in sad and depressing surroundings – depressing at least for you and me – Mother was always full of joy and warmth, and her cheerful attitude helped the Co-Workers. After working with her for some time none of us would be upset at the sight of the sick or the handicapped. Once a visitor watching Mother clean an ugly festering wound said, 'I wouldn't do that for a million dollars.'

Mother sensed the need that children have for love and would hug them tenderly.

'Neither would I,' she said. 'I do it for Jesus.' All of us drew strength from her and were able to work happily to assist the sisters. One of Mother's greatest assets was that she always gave strength to others. At one of the meetings Mother asked, 'During the time you devote to working for the poor I would like you to sacrifice food.' From then on we only had a glass of water if we were thirsty, or perhaps a coffee. We were all very happy to do this and fulfilling this simple request made us all feel even stronger. Her humility and desire to live as simply as the poor coloured every aspect of her life. When she was awarded the Nobel Peace Prize in Oslo she requested that the traditional banquet for the prize be cancelled so that everybody could sacrifice their meal for the poor.

In this book I want to show Mother as I saw her, always happy and full of love. A practical person, she never wanted us to give up our comforts to serve the poor. She never demanded any time from us but stressed that the Co-Workers should first attend to their families and only after that work with the Missionaries of Charity.

She had the unique gift of inspiring faith in all. Most of us who helped her belonged to other faiths. On the occasion of the Silver Jubilee of the Missionaries of Charity she celebrated the event with prayers in churches, temples, mosques and gurdwaras (Sikh temples), with people belonging to all faiths. She met everybody at the same level; no matter how important the person was, she took no account of his position.

Over the years we became very close and I would often talk to her in the evenings before she retired. Sadly, sadly, I miss the kindly voice in which she always answered the telephone. She was indeed more than an icon, a saint.

Nothing escaped her eyes. She must have noticed my clothes over a period of time. One day she asked me with a twinkle in her eyes, 'What will I do with that black coat they gave me to wear for the Templeton Award? I'll give it to you. It's very fashionable, you know.' She had an impish sense of humour, which she retained even when she was gravely ill. She often said that hers was the only business that the government would never nationalize.

I am so glad that Mother got to see my paintings of her, those that I did just a few months before she passed away. 'Where are my eyes?' she would innocently ask. A sister would say to her, 'Mother, this is abstract art.' 'Oh,' she would reply

without further questioning. I imagine her now to be among the most fragrant and lovely of all the flowers that bloom in the valleys.

Every time Mother fell seriously ill I felt a deep urge to be at her bedside to tend to her. She forbade the sisters to call a doctor. Mother was always reluctant to move into 'five-star' hospitals or nursing homes, because she wanted to be treated as the poor would be. She would accept medical help most hesitatingly and only when bullied into it, thinking that if she recovered quickly she would be able to get to China and set up a home there. China became an obsession with her and the Lord granted her last wish when Hong Kong, where she already had a home, became part of China.

It is rare in human history to find anyone with her perseverance, strength and stamina. Imagine a life with every minute, every hour devoted to prayer or serving the poor. She never took a holiday, saying instead, 'We rest in Heaven.' She stood for love and peace, and has left a legacy for many generations to come.

On many occasions we received gifts and notes from her. These are now my most cherished possessions. The wonderful memories of our many years as Mother's devoted family will never die. How fortunate we were to have had such a close and unique bond with her.

LEFT
Mother kissing the miraculous medal. She would then hand the medal to the sick and ask them to pray.

Mother Teresa with the author and her family.

17

MOTHER TERESA'S

EARLY YEARS

Mother Teresa was born Agnes Bojaxhiu in Skopje in Northern Macedonia (now Albania) on 26 August 1910. She was the youngest of three children born to Drana (Rosa) and Kole (Nicholas), a merchant. She had an elder sister, Age, and an elder brother, Lazar.

Agnes was baptized the day after her birth, on 27 August, and a church now stands at the site of her baptism.

When Agnes told her mother that she felt that God was calling her to a life dedicated completely to Him, Drana encouraged her with the advice: 'My daughter, if you begin something, begin it wholeheartedly or don't begin it at all ... daughter, go with my blessing.' On the Feast of the Assumption in 1928 Agnes, aged eighteen, joined the pilgrimage to Letnice for the last time to ask for blessing from the Blessed Mother as she prepared to leave Skopje. On 26 September of the same year Mother left for Ireland to join the novitiate of the Institute of the Blessed Virgin Mary at Loreto Abbey, Dublin, as a postulant.

Two months later, on 29 November 1928, she arrived in Calcutta: 'I observed the life in the streets with strange feelings. Most of the Indians were half naked, their skin and hair glistening in the hot sun. Clearly there was a great poverty among them.' After two years of novitiate in India Sister Teresa took her vows on 24 May 1931. She wrote to her aunt: 'I am fit and well. I send you this photograph as a memento of the greatest day of my life; that on which I became wholly Christ's.'

Sister Teresa then worked in St Mary's Bengali Medium School, Loreto, Entally, Calcutta. St Mary's was primarily for teaching orphans, the homeless and the poor, but also had a section for training primary-school teachers. Sister Teresa had learned to speak fluent Hindi and Bengali and was an outstanding teacher. For the

RIGHT
Mother Teresa (left),
born Agnes
Bojaxhiu, and her
sister in Albanian
dress c. 1928.

Mother signed up to join a Catholic youth group in the Jesuit parish of the Sacred Heart in her home town of Skopje. She had a soprano voice and used to sing in the parish choir. She is seen here third from the right in the middle row.

next few years she was a teacher at St Mary's, which was supported by charitable donations as well as help from the government.

On 24 May 1937 Sister Teresa took her final vows in Loreto Convent, Darjeeling, and from that time she was called Mother Teresa. She returned to St Mary's in 1938 and in 1944 she became Principal there, acquiring valuable leadership qualities.

In the meantime she was in charge of St Teresa's Primary Bengali Medium School on Lower Circular Road, but she would return to Entally every evening. It may have been the Great Famine in Bengal (1943) and its aftermath, or the distress of the poor children in St Teresa's School and in Calcutta that awoke in Mother Teresa the great desire to do for the poor even more than she was doing at St Mary's.

One of Mother's students later said, 'As a girl what struck me most was to see the presence of Christ in Mother. The way she prayed, walked, talked – everything was different from the other nuns.' On 9 September 1946, while on a train to Darjeeling for a retreat, Mother received what she described as 'a call within a call'. She said: 'The message was very clear: I must leave the convent to help the poor by living among them. This was a command, something to be done, something definite. I knew where I had to be but I did not know how to get there.' When Mother returned to Entally, Calcutta, in October she met Father Van Exem who said, 'When she met me she said, "Read this and let me know what you think of it." After reading her notes he said: "It is the will of God."'

Mother's notes were very clear: somebody had spoken to her asking for a society working in poverty and cheerfulness in the streets of Calcutta – no institutions – for the abandoned, those who had nobody. Pope Pius XII granted permission for Mother to leave Loreto on 12 April 1948. However, Father Van Exem prepared the decree for Mother to sign only four months later, on 8 August 1948. Mother remained *Mother as a pretty* bound by her vows, but she now owed her obedience to the Archbishop of Calcutta *young girl with* instead of to her Superior at Loreto. *beautiful eyes in*

On 18 August 1948 Mother Teresa said goodbye to the community of Loreto *Skopje, 25* Convent, Entally, and, donning a white sari with a blue border, she went out in pure *September 1928.* faith. She went first to the hospital of the Medical Missionary Sisters in Patna to do a short course in nursing and dispensary work before actually starting her new mission. She then returned to Calcutta on 8 December 1948 to the Covent of the Little Sisters of the Poor. There Mother made her retreat alone and began her work. That same year she took Indian citizenship and went for the first time to the slums of Taratolla where she rented two rooms in Moti Jhil for five rupees, the amount the Archbishop had given her when she left Loreto. One of the rooms served as a school and the other as the first home for sick and dying destitutes, Nirmal Hriday.

21

LEFT
Mother left her beloved Skopje and entered the novitiate of the Institute of the Blessed Virgin Mary at Loreto Abbey, Rathfarnham, Dublin, as a postulant on 12 October 1928.

On 1 December 1928 Mother sailed for India with Sister Magdalene Kanje (who was also from Yugoslavia) and Sister Joan Berchmans Joyce from Ireland. She arrived on 6 January 1929, the Feast of the Epiphany, which means 'manifestation of the Lord'.

In Moti Jhil she had a group of children to whom she taught Bengali and gave lessons in personal hygiene. She also started a dispensary at St Teresa's School. She would beg for medicine from shopkeepers, and voluntary helpers came to assist her. She saw that many of the poor families did not have even one decent meal a day, so she began to collect leftovers from families in the adjoining street.

In the meantime, Father Henry and Father Van Exem were still looking for a permanent place for Mother; then the Gomes brothers, Michael and Alfred, agreed to take her into their house at 14 Creek Lane. The first two months found her generally alone and overwhelmed with doubts. The endless woes of the poor, the sick and the dying filled her days. Her diary notes her struggle:

'Our Lord wants me to be a free nun covered with the poverty of the cross. Today I learned a good lesson. The poverty of the poor must be so hard for them. While looking for a home [as a centre] I walked and walked until my arms and legs ached. I thought how much they must ache in body and soul, looking for home, food and help. Then the comfort of Loreto came to tempt me. But of my free choice, O my God, and out of love for You, I choose to remain and do whatever is Your Holy Will.'

The first aim of Mother's prayers and planning was to find sisters who would dedicate themselves to this work. Permission was obtained from the Vatican for the foundation of the Order of the Missionaries of Charity on 7 October 1950. Father Van Exem read the Decree of Election during Mass in the chapel on Greek Lane and on 11 April 1951 the first group of sisters entered their novitiate – all except Mother, who had already taken her vows. The first twelve were:

1. Mother
2. Sister M Agnes
3. Sister M Gertrude
4. Sister M Trinita
5. Sister M Dorothy
6. Sister M Clare
7. Sister M Bernard
8. Sister M Laetitia
9. Sister M Jacinta
10. Sister M Francesca
11. Sister M Florence
12. Sister M Margaret Mary

Since then the order has established itself in over 125 countries with 602 homes and 3,914 sisters to date. Numerous awards were bestowed on Mother Teresa during her lifetime for her untiring work; in 1979 she received the Nobel Peace Prize and in 1980 she received the Bharat Ratna, the highest Indian award.

In 1937 Mother professed permanent vows in Darjeeling, about six thousand feet up in the Himalayas. She took the name 'Teresa' and returned to Calcutta as a Loreto nun.

Lazar Bojaxhiu, Mother Teresa, Maria, Agi, her husband Beppe and Sister Nirmala.

After thirty years Mother met her brother Lazar in February 1967 in Rome. She was meeting his wife Maria and their daughter Agi (then twenty-one) for the first time. Agi, who now lives near Palermo with her husband, said that this was 'a very moving meeting'. Mother told us that when her brother Lazar, who was an officer in the army, found out that she was becoming a nun he was very surprised. 'Do you know what you are doing?' he asked, to which Mother replied: 'I'm an officer too, but in the service of the king of the world.'

Mother visits her niece Agi and her grand-nephew Dominico near Palermo in 1990.

BELOW Massimilliano (her grand-nephew), Beppe, Agi and Dominico with Mother Teresa near Palermo in 1987.

THE MISSIONARIES
OF CHARITY

The Missionaries of Charity is an international religious family with active and contemplative branches taking perpetual public vows of chastity, poverty and obedience, and whole-hearted and free service to the poorest of the poor – leading each person to the perfect love of God and their neighbour, making the Church fully present in the world of today.

The society is dedicated to the Immaculate Heart of Mary, Cause of Joy and Queen of the World. The spirit of the society is one of total surrender, loving trust and cheerfulness.

The mother house and centre of training is at 54A, Acharya Jagdish Chandra Bose Road, Calcutta 700016. There are also training centres in other parts of India and in different continents – Europe, the Americas, Asia, Africa and Australasia.

Every member of the society goes where she is sent and does not choose her place of work or the kind of work she would like to do. They go out in pairs and say the rosary daily at home and on their way to and from their work. The language of the society is English.

RIGHT

An unending stream of poor people seek her help for medicine, food, shelter and advice on their domestic problems.

DAILY ROUTINE

4.40 a.m.	Rise
5 a.m.	Morning prayer and meditation
6 a.m.	Holy Mass
6.45 a.m.	Breakfast
7.10 a.m.	Laundry and housework
8 a.m. to 12 noon	Apostolate. Sisters go out to the different homes, street dispensaries, etc.
12.15 a.m.	The sisters all return
12.30 p.m.	Lunch
1.10 p.m.	Examination prayer
1.30 to 2 p.m.	Rest
2 p.m.	Spiritual reading
2.45 to 6 p.m.	Apostolate
6.10 p.m.	Divine office
6.30 to 7.30 p.m.	Holy Hour – Adoration
7.30 p.m.	Supper
8.10 p.m.	Free time
8.30 to 9 p.m.	Recreation
9 to 9.20 p.m.	Night prayers
10 p.m.	Bedtime

On Thursdays and Sundays Adoration is at 6 p.m. and supper at 7 p.m.

Mother inspecting the cleanliness of a room. All her homes are regularly scrubbed and kept clean.

THE RELIGIOUS

CONSECRATED LIFE

As a sign of entering into a new state of life and of desire for self-effacement:
- you receive a new religious name at Profession
- you call each other 'sister'
- your hair is cut off.

The religious dress consists of:
- a simple and modest white cotton habit
- a white cotton sari with blue border covering the head
- a cincture made of rope
- a pair of sandals
- a crucifix and rosary.

It is considered an honour and privilege to serve Christ in the distressing disguise of the poorest of the poor doing humble work using humble means and relying on the omnipotence of God, Who said 'Without me you can do nothing.'

The religious training of candidates extends over four years:
- aspirancy: 1 year and longer if necessary
- postulancy: 1 year
- novitiate: 2 years.

Work

The special aim of the society is to labour at the salvation and sanctification of the poorest of the poor, not only in the slums but also all over the world wherever they may be by:
- nursing sick and dying destitutes
- gathering and teaching little street children
- visiting and caring for beggars, leprosy patients and their children
- giving shelter to the abandoned and homeless
- caring for the unwanted, the unloved and the lonely.

This is achieved by means of:

- homes for abandoned and crippled children, Shishu Bhavan
- homes for sick and dying destitutes, Nirmal Hriday
- mobile clinics, leprosy clinics and leprosy rehabilitation centres
- primary schools in the slums, sewing, handicraft and typing classes
- going out to the spiritually poorest of the poor to proclaim the Word of God by the presence of sisters and spiritual works of mercy
- and by Adoration of Jesus in the Blessed Sacrament.

Candidates desirous to join the society must be:

- at least eighteen years of age
- guided by the right intention
- healthy in body and mind and able to bear the hardships of this vocation
- able to acquire knowledge, especially the language of the people they serve
- of a cheerful disposition
- able to exercise sound judgement.

Mother with the Head Priest of the Kali Temple, which is situated next to Nirmal Hriday, her Home for the Dying. She invited him to meet the Holy Father when he visited Nirmal Hriday.

BELOW With Sister Agnes on her daily mission of mercy in the teeming streets of Calcutta.
Regularly they would visit the slums and help the poor in whatever manner they could.

ABOVE RIGHT Mother fought abortion with
adoption. She would say, 'If you prefer not
to have it, don't kill it – give it to me.'

BELOW RIGHT 'The greatest poverty in the world is not the want of
food but the want of love. You have the poverty of people who are
dissatisfied with what they have, who do not know how to suffer,
who give in to despair. The poverty of the heart is often more
difficult to relieve and to defeat.'

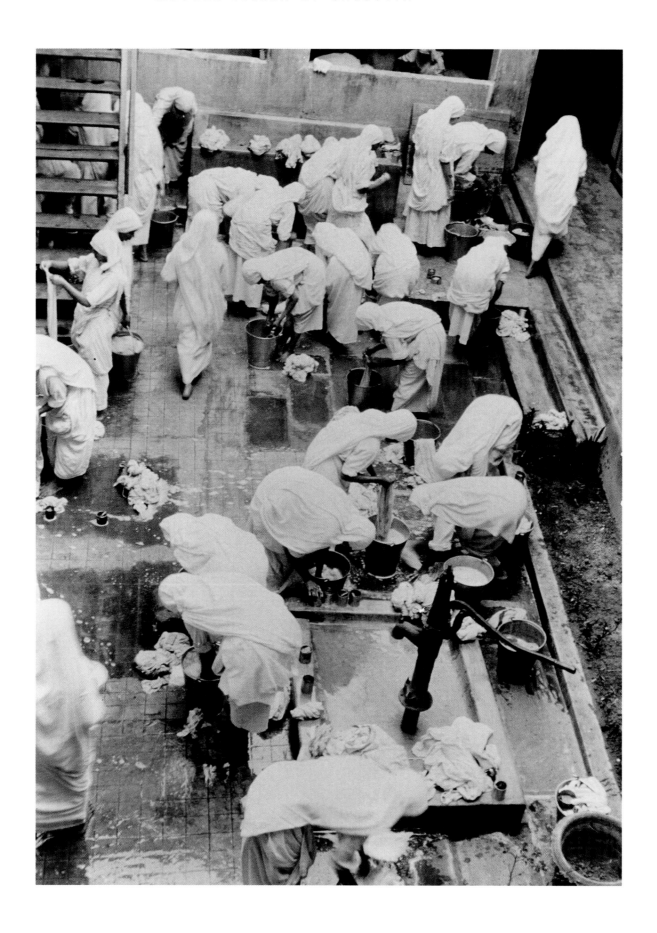

Mother Teresa sending the novices out to their work. The sisters always move about in pairs – they never go out alone.

LEFT

Novices washing clothes. This is a familiar scene every morning after breakfast in the courtyard at Mother's house. Within an hour the whole area is spotlessly clean and dry, and the clothes are put out to dry on the roof.

LEFT
Mother Teresa at
work on the streets
of Calcutta.

ABOVE RIGHT
To the orphaned
and unwanted
children she gave
food, shelter and
love. Most of
them are adopted
by good families.
The others are
educated and given
vocational training.

BELOW RIGHT
Mother often visited
government offices
to expedite her
work. Wherever she
went a crowd
invariably collected
to receive her
blessings.

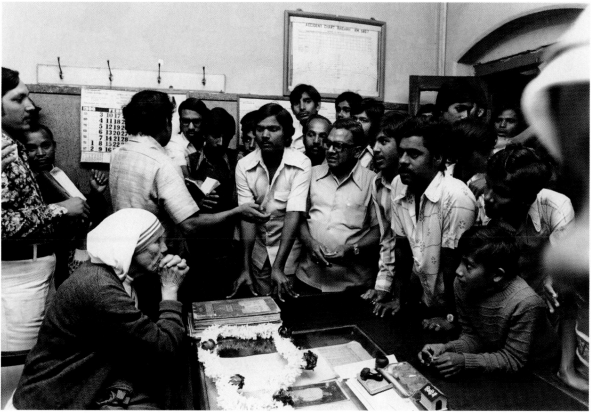

Mother signing some letters in her strong, firm handwriting.

'I am a little pencil in God's hands. He does the thinking. He does the writing. He does everything and sometimes it is really hard because it is a broken pencil and He has to sharpen it a little more. Be a little instrument in His hands so that He can use you any time, anywhere. We have only to say "yes" to God.'

LEFT

Mother Teresa ventures out on the streets of Calcutta during a bandh (a total stoppage of everything) in 1992. Her work, however, never stopped and she went about it without fear.

*Mother Teresa comforting one of the inmates of Nirmal
Hriday. She would kiss the miraculous medal and hand
it to the sick, asking them to pray 'Mary Mother of Jesus
be a Mother to me now.' Many miracles happened.*

LEFT

*What's going on
here? How can I
help? She had a
one-track mind.*

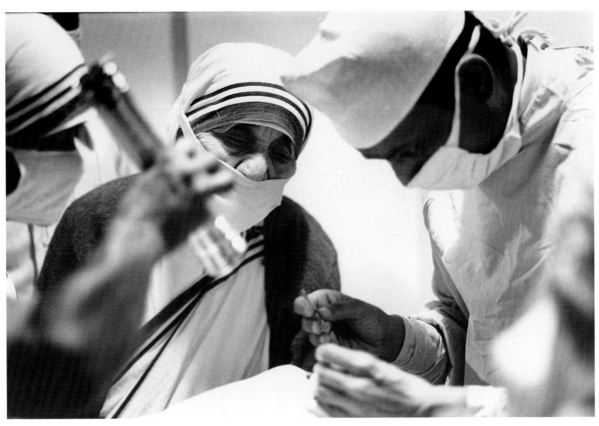

A helping hand. This picture epitomizes the work of the Missionaries of Charity.

ABOVE LEFT Sisters cheerfully seeing Mother off when she visited them in one of her homes near Calcutta.

BELOW LEFT At a free eye camp for the poor in a remote village, Mother watches a cataract operation being carried out.

No time to rest. Always on the move, working for the poorest of the poor.

ABOVE LEFT Wherever Mother went people touched
her feet to receive her blessings.

BELOW LEFT Mother said, 'It is not how much we do,
but how much love we put in the doing. It is not how
much we give, but how much love we put in the giving.'

Mother Teresa
walking down the
lane leading to her
home. She was a
tireless worker.

People from all
walks of life and
different faiths
sought her
blessings.

RIGHT

With the Co-Workers at a Christmas party
for children from Mother's homes.

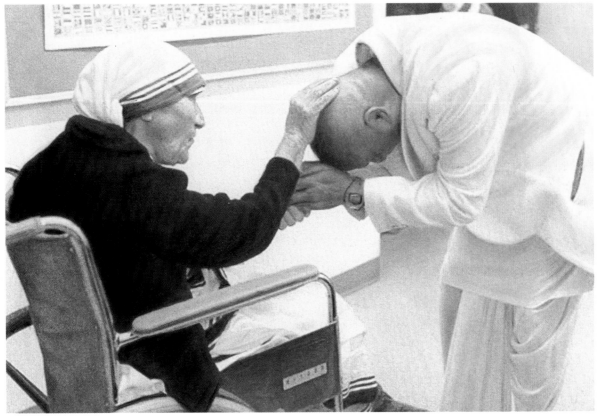

ABOVE

With the Missionaries of Charity brothers on her last visit to Rome.

RIGHT

Mother at Raigarh Church where she attended a Sunday sermon in 1980.

LEFT

Mother praying with the miraculous medal. She always said, 'Your prayers will be answered.'

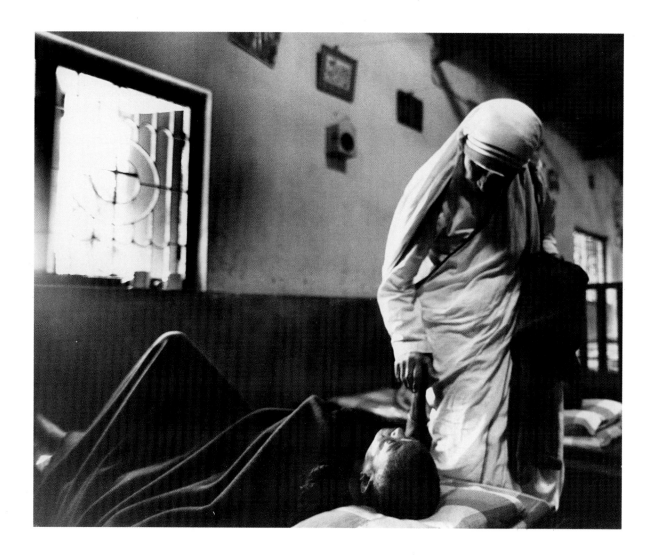

'We do nothing. He does everything. All glory must be returned to Him. God had not called me to be successful. He had called me to be faithful.'

'We must not drift away from the humble works, because these are the works nobody will do. They are never too small. We are so small we look at things in a small way. Even if we do a small thing for somebody, God, being almighty, sees everything as great. For there are people who can do big things. But there are very few people who will do the small things.'

'None of us, I am sure, knows what is the pain of hunger, but one day I learned it from a little child. I found that child in the street and I saw in her face that terrible hunger that I have seen in many eyes. Without questioning her I gave her a piece of bread, and then I saw the little child was eating the bread crumb by crumb. And I said to her, "Eat the bread". And that little one looked to me and said, "I am afraid because when the bread is finished I will be hungry again."'

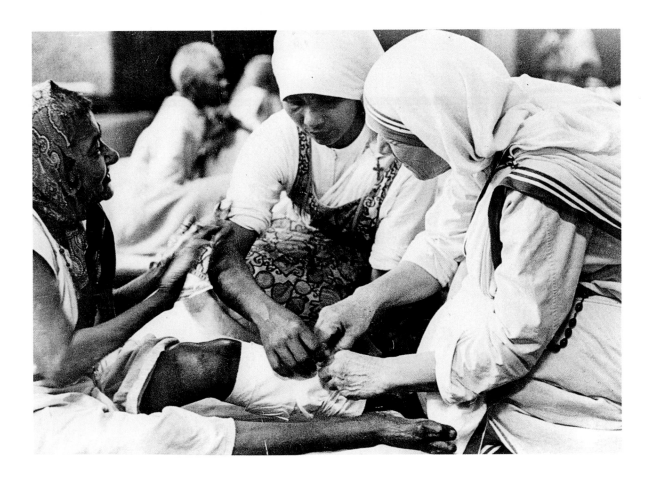

Mother bandaging a leper's leg. She would often say, 'I can do what you can't do. You can do what I can't do. Together we can do something beautiful for God.'

Mother looking after a crippled child.

'"You did it to me." This is the only reason and the joy of my life: to love and serve Him in the distressing disguise of the poor, the unwanted, the hungry, the thirsty, the naked, the homeless, and naturally in so doing, I proclaim His love and compassion for each one of my suffering brothers and sisters.'

'There is much suffering in the world – but I still think that the greatest suffering is being lonely, feeling unloved, just having no one.'

In her home called Prem Dan, which means gift of love.

'The poor must know that we love them, that they are wanted. They
themselves have nothing to give but love. We are concerned with
how to get this message across. We are trying to bring peace to
the world through our work. But the work is the gift of God.'

Volunteers come from all over the world to work at Mother's homes in Calcutta.

'I don't want that you give from your abundance. I want you to understand through direct contact. The poor need deeds, not words.'

Mother Teresa would go to Kalighat, the House for the Dying, and the first thing she would do there was to clean the toilets – a humble work of love.

'Speak tenderly to them. Let there be kindness in your face, in your eyes, in your smile, in the warmth of your greeting. Always have a cheerful smile. Don't only give your care, but give your heart as well.'

'No colour, no religion, no nationality should come between us.
We are all the children of God.'

ABOVE LEFT
One can feel the strength in Mother's firm
hand as she bolsters a sick man's confidence.

BELOW LEFT
Mother was able to reach out to the old and
the young, and had a special affinity with
children.

PRAYER

The Missionaries of Charity have a rule to devote half an hour a day to spiritual reading. It comprises reading a couple of rules from the Constitution and a passage from the New Testament, or a book on the life of the saints or on the ascetic life.

Usually Mother would sit at the back of the chapel opposite the altar and the statue of Our Lady. But sometimes she would sit near the window as seen opposite because the light was dim and she chose not to use electricity because of her vow of poverty.

Let us pray for the repose of the soul of our Sister She has been a beautiful example of simple love God bless you M Teresa mc

*Mother genuflecting towards the Blessed Sacrament in the chapel.
The sisters do this before entering and leaving the chapel. It is
similar to bowing before a king because of the faith they have in
Jesus's real presence in the Blessed Eucharist, and it shows respect.
Usually when they genuflect they say a little prayer.*

*Mother praying from the Missionaries of
Charity prayer book. She is totally
engrossed. She loved every word of the
prayers and when she prayed each word
was a living work for her.*

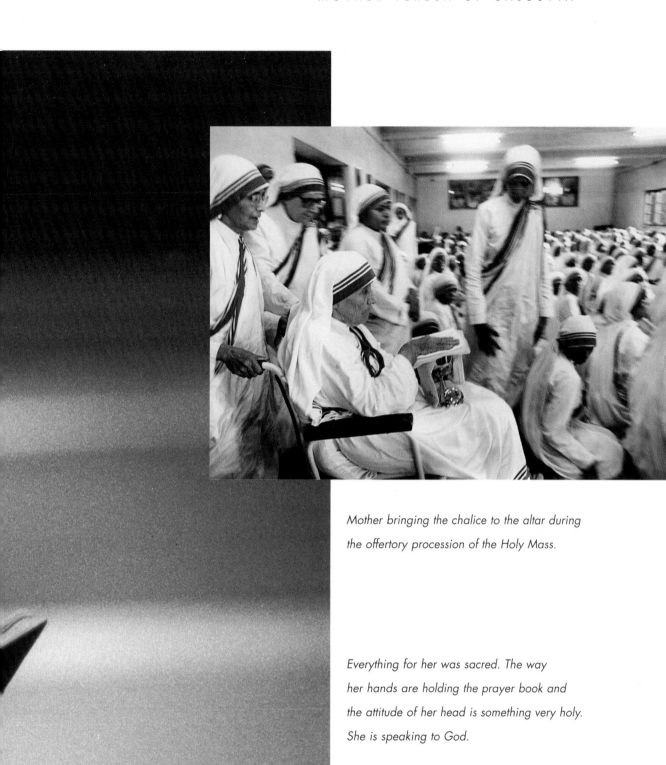

Mother bringing the chalice to the altar during
the offertory procession of the Holy Mass.

Everything for her was sacred. The way
her hands are holding the prayer book and
the attitude of her head is something very holy.
She is speaking to God.

Mother travelling on a train to Raigarh. She is making the half-hour meditation as required by the Missionaries of Charity. She was always faithful to her prayer, whether she was travelling or not.

Mother kneeling below the picture of her patroness, Saint Thérèse of Liseux. The words in the picture 'Confidence and nothing but confidence' are the motif of this saint. Mother's spirituality was very much based on the spirituality of Saint Thérèse, which can be seen as a spirituality of confidence in and love for God.

71

At the reading of the gospel at Holy Mass, when the congregation stands listening attentively. They stand because they believe that they are hearing Jesus speaking through the priest.

LEFT At Holy Communion the sisters kneel in adoration after receiving the Body and Blood, Soul and Divinity of their spouse Jesus Christ.

In her usual place in the chapel in meditation on the Gospel.

LEFT The sister who is standing is making the fourteen Stations of the Cross representing the journey that Jesus took to his death on the cross on Mount Calvary. The other three sisters are visiting Jesus present in the tabernacle.

BELOW
Mother at Holy Communion, totally immersed in the presence of Jesus who has come into her heart.

Novices at prayer.
When you visit
Mother's house you
will always find
sisters or novices in
small groups at
prayer. The sound
of them praying
together or singing
hymns together is
blissfully peaceful.

RIGHT
Mother at prayer.

IMPORTANT DATES IN
MOTHER TERESA'S LIFE

26/8/1910	Birth in Skopje
27/8/1910	Baptism
16/11/1916	Confirmation
25/9/1928	Departure from Skopje to enter the Loreto Postulancy in Rathfarnham, Dublin
29/11/1928	Departure from Ireland for India
6/1/1929	Arrival in Calcutta to begin her novitiate in Darjeeling
23/5/1929	Entrance into the novitiate
24/5/1931	First profession in Darjeeling, followed by assignment to St Mary's High School in Calcutta
24/5/1937	Final vows in Loreto, Darjeeling, and return to Calcutta
9/9/1946	Departure by train for retreat in Darjeeling
10/9/1946	Inspiration Day
16/8/1948	Separation from Loreto, departure for Patna to stay with Medical Missionary Sisters for three months
8/12/1948	Return to Calcutta to stay temporarily with the Little Sisters of the Poor
21/12/1948	Opening of first slum school in Moti Jhil
1948	Became an Indian citizen
2/1/1949	Writing of the first rule
2/2/1949	Move to 14 Creek Lane, Michael Gomes's house
19/3/1949	Subhasini Das (Sister M. Agnes, MC) became the first to join Mother
7/10/1950	Approval of the foundation of the Order of Missionaries of Charity by Pope Pius XII
11/4/1951	First group of sisters enter novitiate
22/8/1952	Opening of Nirmal Hriday, Home for the Dying, Kalighat, Calcutta

Mother in Rome in 1971 when Pope Paul VI presented her with the Peace Prize established by Pope John XXIII.

12/4/1953	First profession of the first group of the Missionaries of Charity
29/5/1959	Foundation at Ranchi, first mission house outside Calcutta
7/10/1961	First chapter general
4/1962	Padma Shri Award in New Delhi
31/8/1962	Ramon Magsaysay Award for spreading international understanding, Manila, Philippines
25/3/1963	Foundation of Missionary Brothers of Charity (Active)
12/1964	Eucharistic Congress. Pope Paul VI donated a car at the Eucharistic Congress in Bombay
1/2/1965	Decree of Praise by Pope Paul VI
6/1/1971	Pope John XXIII Peace Prize awarded by Paul VI, Vatican City
25/6/1976	Foundation of Missionaries of Charity, Contemplative Branch, in New York
19/3/1979	Foundation of Missionaries of Charity, Contemplative Brothers, in Rome
10/12/1979	Nobel Peace Prize, Oslo, Norway
22/3/1980	Bharat Ratna Award (the highest Indian award), New Delhi
28/6/1980	(Cert.) Meritorious Citizen of Skopje
31/10/1984	Foundation of Missionary Fathers of Charity in New York

Since then Mother Teresa has received so many awards, medals, citations, keys to cities, and other forms of recognition of her great work that it is not possible to include them all here.

BELOW RIGHT Mother Teresa received the Nobel Peace Prize on 10 December 1979.

'I choose the poverty of our poor people. But I am grateful to receive [the Nobel] in the name of the hungry, the naked, the homeless, of the crippled, of the blind, of the lepers, of all those people who feel unwanted, unloved, uncared for throughout society, people that have become a burden to the society and are shunned by everyone.'

Mother presents Sister Nirmala to the Holy Father as the Superior General of the Order. At the time she said, 'Holy Father, she's the Superior General. I am completely free now.' To which he replied, 'You still remain the foundress.'

Mother visits the Holy Father in Vatican City, in December 1979 after receiving the Nobel Peace Prize, before she returned to Calcutta.

Pope John Paul II presents Mother with the keys of a building in Rome in 1980. It is now a home for unmarried mothers.

Mother Teresa being decorated with the highest Indian award, the Bharat Ratna ('Jewel of India'), by the President, Mr N Sanjiviya Reddy, at Rashtrapati Bhavan in New Delhi on 22 March 1980.

Mother with the late Satyajit Ray at Jadavpur University Convocation, where she received the D. Lit.

In a gurdwara at Calcutta. Mother transcended religion. She said, 'There is only one God and He is God to all; therefore it is important that everyone is seen as equal before God. I've always said we should help a Hindu become a better Hindu, a Muslim become a better Muslim, a Catholic become a better Catholic.'

RIGHT
Mother with the Holy Father. After one of her visits she wrote to the sisters: 'The Holy Father will bless each one of you and obtain for you the graces you need to become saints.'

Mother arrives in New Mexico to establish a new foundation in Gallop to work with the American Indians in 1983. She is accompanied by Sister Frederick, the late Bishop of New Mexico and a close friend, Sandy McMurtrie.

ABOVE & RIGHT
When Pope John
Paul II visited Nirmal
Hriday, her Home
for the Dying, in
1986, Mother held
his hand and led
him in. She was
delighted when he
said he would like
a home for the poor
in the Vatican and
in 1988 Mother
started a home for
poor elderly women
there.

'For me, life is the most beautiful gift of God to mankind, therefore people and nations who destroy life by abortion and euthanasia are the poorest. I do not say legal or illegal, but I think that no human hand should be raised to kill life, since life is God's life in us, even in an unborn child.'

In 1991 Mother meets the Holy Father on her way back to Calcutta from South America, where she had received surgical attention. The Holy Father received her affectionately and wished her a speedy recovery.

Mother shows the Holy Father papers regarding her visit to Vietnam in 1994.

Sister Agnes, who was the first one to join Mother on 19 March 1949, passed away on 9 April 1997. Mother, who was seriously ill herself, insisted on going to the burial.

'Let us pray for the repose of the soul of our sister. She has been a beautiful example of a simple love. God bless you.'

The Congressional Medal was presented to Mother Teresa by the Members of the Congress of the United States in Washington DC in May 1997.

Mother blesses Sister Nirmala on the balcony at the Mother House.

'I am grateful from my heart to each one of you for all the love, care and help you have all given me during these years. With your help, I have been able to do something beautiful for God. Let us continue the beautiful work to serve the Poorest of the Poor with great love and care.'

At one of her meetings with the press. Mother Teresa was always smiling.

Keep the joy of
loving the Poor
and share this joy
with all you meet
Remember
Works of love are
Works of Peace
God bless you
Mc Teresa mc

MOTHER TERESA 1910–97

1 October 1996. This was the only time that I saw Mother in bed in her room. She was very unwell on her feast day and allowed me and two Co-Workers, Amita Mitter and Sylvia Luddy, to spend time with her.

Mother returning home from the hospital in December 1996. She always sat in the front seat.

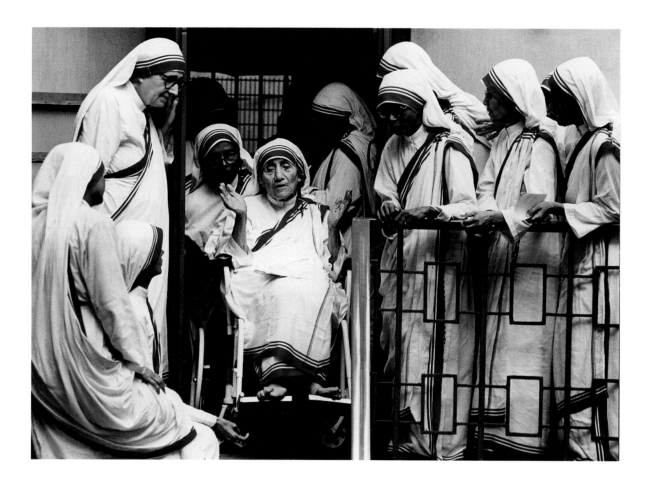

Mother with her flock of loving sisters, only a few months before she passed away.

26 August 1997. With Sister Gertrude, Sister Luke and Sister Nirmala on the balcony of the Mother House acknowledging the birthday wishes of the crowd in the courtyard.

A Muslim inmate at Nirmal Hriday praying for Mother's recovery when she was critically ill in 1997.

A passer-by prays for Mother's recovery outside her home when she was very ill.

At the door of the Mother house. I am announcing Mother's going home to Jesus to the press, 5 September 1997.

Mother lies in the sacristy at the feet of Lady Fatima. She was moved from the chapel to this room where all the religious relics were kept as it was easier for everyone to see her in the sacristy.

One last glimpse of Mother was all they wanted and needed.

People waited for hours in serpentine queues.

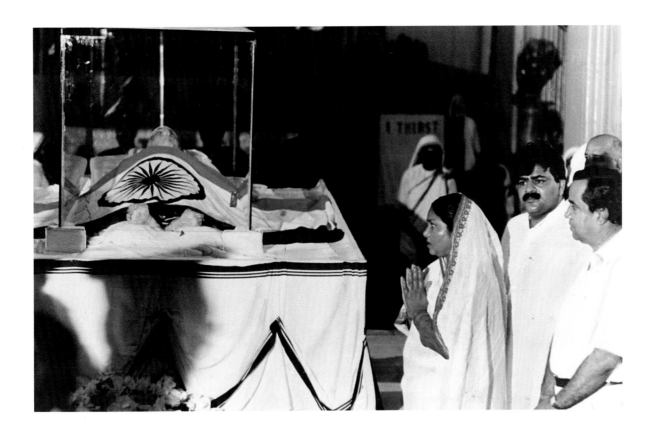

Phoolan Devi pays homage to Mother. Known as 'the Bandit Queen', Phoolan's life story is portrayed in the film of the same name.

RIGHT All work came to a stop. Thousands lined the procession route to see and pay respects to Mother on her last journey.

The route of the funeral procession had to be extended to accommodate the thousands who wanted to pay their respects on her last journey. Here her cortège passes by the Victoria Memorial. The gun carriage is the same one that had carried the bodies of Mahatma Gandhi and Jawaharlal Nehru.

The funeral procession.

A solemn moment as Mother is brought into the Stadium.
Dignitaries, friends and associates came from all over the world
for the funeral. Not a single room was available in Calcutta.

*Cardinal Sodano, Secretary of State of the Vatican, represented
the Holy Father at the funeral mass concelebrated by the
Archbishop of Calcutta, Henry D'Souza.*

The Holy Father's representative, along with the other bishops and cardinals, gives the final blessing to Mother.

*From left to right: Mrs Hillary Clinton, Mrs
Chretien, the wife of the Prime Minister of
Canada, and Mrs Sonia Gandhi.*

*Mr Jyoti Basu, Chief Minister of West Bengal, pays his last respects
to Mother Teresa. Mother was fond of him and after hearing the
news he said, 'I had known her since 1975. After we came to
power we had given her help in her work. She helped us by taking
charge of abandoned girls whom we had to shelter in our jails.
I am deeply grieved at the demise of such a great humanitarian.'*

Sisters during Adoration near Mother's tomb.

Mother's tomb. It has become a place of pilgrimage and the sisters go there for Adoration and Mass. People of all religions sit by the tomb and pray. Some come with petitions and many receive answers to their prayers.

MOTHER TERESA'S
FAVOURITE HYMNS

O JESUS, JESUS, DEAREST LORD

O Jesus, Jesus, dearest Lord
Forgive me if I say
For very love Thy Sacred Name
A thousand times a day.

I love Thee so, I know not how
My transports to control.
Thy love is like a burning fire
Within my very soul.

O wonderful that Thou shouldst let
So vile a heart as mine
Love Thee with such a love as this
And make so free with Thine.

For Thou to me are all in all
My honour and my wealth,
My heart's desire, my body's strength
My soul's eternal health.

What limit is there to Thee, love?
Thy flight where wilt Thou stay?
On! On! Our lord is sweeter far
Today than yesterday.

LORD JESUS

Lord Jesus of you I will sing as I journey
I'll tell all my brothers about you wherever I go;
You alone are man's life and his peace and his love.
Lord Jesus of you I will sing as I journey.

Lord Jesus I'll praise you as long as I journey.
May all of my joy be a faithful reflection of you.
May the earth and the sea and the sky join my song.
Lord Jesus I'll praise you as long as I journey.

As long as I live, Jesus make me your servant.
To carry your cross and to share all your burdens and tears.
For you saved me by giving your body and blood.
As long as I live, Jesus make me your servant.

I fear in the dark and the doubt of my journey,
But courage will come with the sound of your steps by my side
And with all of my brothers you saved by your love
We'll sing to your dawn at the end of our journey.

O WHAT COULD MY JESUS DO MORE

O what could my Jesus do more,
Or what greater blessing impart.
O silence my soul and adore,
And press Him still nearer Thy Heart.
'Tis here from my labours I'll rest
Since He makes my poor heart His abode.
To Him all my cares I'll address,
And speak to the heart of my God.

In life and in death Thou art mine,
My Saviour I'm saved with Thy blood.
Till eternity on me doth shine
I'll live on the flesh of my God.
In Jesus Triumphant I'll live,
In Jesus Triumphant I'll die.
The terrors of death calmly brave.
In His bosom breathe out my last sigh.

MOTHER OF GOD'S HOLY CHILD

Mother of God's little Child,
    I am little, too.
Guide my step and clear my path;
    lead me home to you.
You're my mother, too; I depend on you
I am little like your little Child.

Mother of God's precious Child,
    I am precious too.
He grew up and died for me
    and He gave me you.
You're my mother, too;
    I belong to you;
I am precious like your
    precious Child.

Mother of God's holy Child
    make me holy, too.
Keep my heart from every wrong;
    keep it close to you.
You're my mother, too;
    I will trust in you;
Make me holy like your holy Child.

ONLY A SHADOW

The love I have for You my Lord
Is only a shadow of Your love for me
Only a shadow of Your Love for me
Your deep abiding love.

My own belief in You, my Lord
Is only a shadow of Your faith in me
Only a shadow of Your faith in me
Your deep and lasting faith.

My life is in Your hands
My life is in Your hands
My love for You will grow, my God
Your light in me will shine.

The dream I have today, my Lord
Is only a shadow of Your dreams for me.
Only a shadow of all that will be
If I but follow You.

The joy I feel today, my Lord
Is only a shadow of Your joys for me
Only a shadow of Your joys for me
When we meet face to face.

My life is in Your hands
My life is in Your hands
My love for You will grow, my God
Your light in me will shine.

When Jesus was dying on the cross, He cried out 'I thirst.' Mother was inspired to write 'Our aim is to quench the infinite thirst of Jesus Christ on the Cross for the love of souls...', and the constitution of the Missionaries of Charity states, 'We quench the thirst of Jesus by the profession of the evangelical councils (chastity, poverty and obedience) and wholehearted and free service to the poorest of the poor.' This is the gift of the Holy Spirit to Mother for the church and the world.

COUNTRIES WHERE THE MISSIONARIES OF CHARITY ARE BASED

United Kingdom	Armenia	Uganda	Nicaragua
England	Georgia	Tanzania	Honduras
Scotland	Tajikistan	Seychelles	El Salvador
Northern Ireland	Lithuania	Central African	Venezuela
Wales	Estonia	Republic	Grenada
Ireland	Belorussia	Cameroon	Trinidad & Tobago
Iceland	Uzbekistan	Democratic Republic	Guyana
Germany	Kazakhstan	of Congo (Zaire)	Santa Lucia
Belgium	Latvia	Ivory Coast	Ecuador
Holland	Mongolia	Ghana	Bolivia
Austria	Jordan	Congo	Peru
Croatia	Palestine	Sierra Leone	Colombia
Slovenia	Syria	Guinea	Brazil
Sweden	Lebanon	Liberia	Paraguay
Denmark	Yemen	Benin	Uruguay
Italy	Iraq	Nigeria	Argentina
Vatican City	Egypt	Gambia	Chile
Spain	Malta	Niger	Philippines
Portugal	Libya	Senegal	China (Hong Kong)
France	Sudan	Burkina Faso	Macau
Morocco	Tunisia	USA	Singapore
Switzerland	Ethiopia	Canada	Taiwan
Poland	Djibouti	Mexico	Korea
Romania	Republic of South	Haiti	Japan
Hungary	Africa	Dominican Republic	Cambodia
Czech Republic	Zambia	Jamaica	Australia
Slovakia	Mozambique	Puerto Rico (US	Papua New Guinea
Albania	Madagascar	Commonwealth)	Bangladesh
Greece	Mauritius	Virgin Islands (US	Sri Lanka
Bulgaria	Malawi	Commonwealth)	Pakistan
Yugoslavia	Zimbabwe	Cuba	India
Macedonia	Kenya	Costa Rica	Nepal
Russia	Burundi	Guatemala	
Ukraine	Rwanda	Panama	

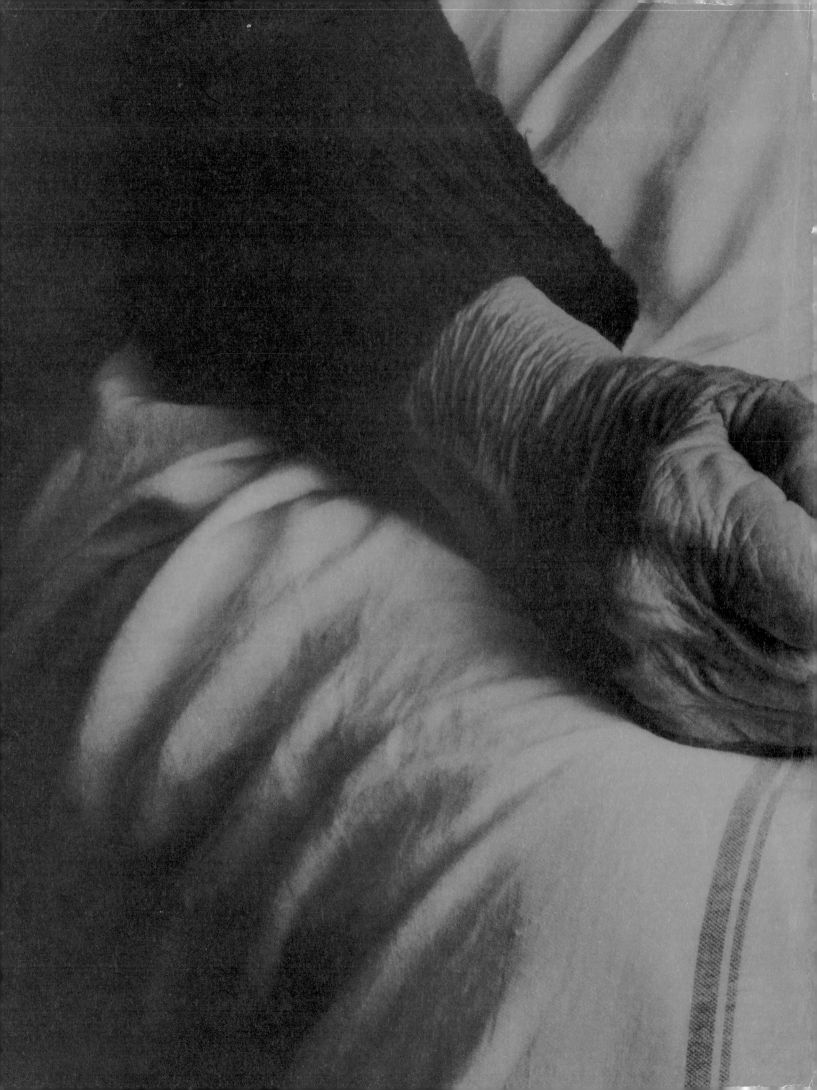